To Jack June '94.

from Susan & Fred.

On Great Northern Lines

Derek Huntriss

First published 1994

ISBN 0 7110 2286 0

Designed by Derek Huntriss

Published by Ian Allan Publishing

An imprint of Ian Allan Ltd, Terminal House, Station Approach, Shepperton, Surrey TW17 8AS; and printed by Ian Allan Printing Ltd., Coombelands House, Coombelands Lane, Addlestone, Weybridge, Surrey KT15 1HY.

Front Cover:
Recently outshopped from Darlington Works after receiving a Casual Light repair, Ex-LNER 'V2' No 60862 crosses the River Idle, south of Retford, with a southbound freight in May 1961. *D. Penney*

Rear Cover:
An up King's Cross suburban train is seen near Brookmans Park on 28 February 1959 behind Thompson 'L1' 2-6-4T No 67780. *T. B. Owen*

This Page:
'A1' Pacific No 60120 *Kittiwake* receives attention at King's Cross whilst it awaits its next turn of duty on 9 November 1957. *T. B. Owen*

Introduction

Of the pre-Grouping railway companies, the Great Northern Railway was one of marked contrasts. Its main line to the capital was celebrated for the grace of its locomotives and trains, and in King´s Cross it possessed what was to many, the finest of the London termini, even to this day remaining majestic despite the unsightly clutter of buildings which have been added to its frontage.

In its early years the company built much of its wealth by securing the transport of the greater part of the coal traffic to the capital in addition to developing fast and regular steam-hauled commuter services to the outer suburbs.

Beyond this, the GNR had embarked on less profitable routes across Nottinghamshire, Lincolnshire and Leicestershire with various branches straggling the northern counties well away from its well-known East Coast main line. Despite the wealth created from traffic originating in the Yorkshire and Nottinghamshire coalfields, the GNR was never a rich concern and lacked the power that wealth had brought to the rival Midland and London and North Western Railways.

In 1911 Herbert Nigel Gresley was chosen to succeed Ivatt as locomotive engineer of the GNR and in the remaining 12 years before the Grouping he developed improved motive power for mixed traffic and freight services. It was to be in the final year of the GNR that he introduced his Class A1 locomotive for hauling the heaviest passenger trains and under the LNER he continued his exciting policies for motive power development right up until the outbreak of war in 1939. Undoubtedly he will always be remembered for his Class A4 Pacifics, in particular for No 4468 *Mallard* which still holds the record for being the world's fastest steam locomotive. Upon his death in April 1941 he was succeeded by Edward Thompson, whose good work in standardising the LNER workshops was clouded by a personal dislike of Gresley design features. His rebuilds never equalled those from which they were derived and fortunately he retired in 1946 thus allowing Peppercorn enough time to retrieve some locomotive prestige for the LNER.

It was locomotives developed in this period that in addition to the BR Class 9F 2-10-0s were to provide the majority of motive power for GNR line services right up to the demise of BR steam.

Presenting the reader with a journey from King´s Cross to Leeds and Bradford, this title depicts in colour the routes of the former GNR system. However, the former GNR secondary routes were amongst the first to succumb to diesel traction and colour photographs of steam operations are almost unknown. However, a small representation of these lines has been included together with two views of former GNR locomotives that have operated in preservation.

Bibliography

Roger Griffiths & John Hooper: *Great Northern Railway Engine Sheds - Vol 1 - Southern Area*; Irwell Press.
P. B. Hands: *What Happened to Steam - Vols 1 to 30*; P. B. Hands.
Chris Hawkins: *The Great British Railway Station - Kings Cross*; Irwell Press.
Peter Hay: *Pre-Grouping Trains on British Railways - The LNER Companies*; Oxford Publishing Company.
O. S. Nock: *Pre-Grouping Railway Scene - Great Northern*; Ian Allan.
Paul Smith: *The Handbook of Steam Motive Power Depots - Vols 1 to 4*; Platform 5 Publishing Co.
P. N. Townend: *The Colour of Steam - Vol 4 - The LNER Pacifics*; Atlantic Transport Publishing Co.
W. B. Yeadon: *Yeadon´s Register of LNER Locomotives - Vols 1 to 5*; Irwell Press.
Magazines: *Trains Illustrated; Backtrack; Railway Magazine; Steam Railway; Steam World; Railway World.*

Acknowledgements

Thanks are offered to all the dedicated photographers whose work appears in these pages. Without their efforts in pioneering the use of slow colour film many years ago and storing their irreplaceable images in good condition over the intervening period, this title could not have been contemplated.

Derek Huntriss   Camborne
Cornwall
November 1993

Right:
A young photographer prepares to capture LNER Class A3 No 60103 *Flying Scotsman* as it backs away from the platforms at King's Cross on 18 August 1962. *G. Rixon*

'A4' No 60022 *Mallard* prepares to leave King's Cross on 8 August 1962. After completing 1,426,261 miles in revenue earning service, No 60022 was withdrawn on 25 April 1963 and entered Doncaster Works for what was believed to be cosmetic restoration before exhibition at Clapham Museum. Contemporary reports suggest that this may have been a diplomatic smokescreen where attention to mechanical parts was to be limited to enable it to be hauled out of steam to London. It is now understood to have received many more repairs, costs being allocated to other jobs. Today, after restoration at the National Railway Museum, York, *Mallard* is one of the museum's notable attractions and was initially returned to steam for the NRM's 10th anniversary celebrations in September 1985. *P. Riley*

Allocated to King's Cross (34A) MPD on 1 November 1959, 'A3' No 60067 *Ladas* arrives in the capital with an up express on 30 April 1962. Although this locomotive was in splendid form and had been fitted with German type smoke deflectors at King's Cross depot in 1961, it was scrapped when due for repair in December 1962. It was the policy at that time to update older locomotives at minimum cost during the changeover to diesel traction. After completing 35,000 miles in traffic after leaving Works, all Class A3 and A4 Pacifics were sent to Doncaster for their valves and pistons to be inspected. This examination would include the valve gear, coupling rods and big ends and the driving pair of axleboxes being renewed. These operations, formerly carried out at King's Cross MPD, saved material being sent in wagons both ways and resulted in a much quicker turnround of the locomotive and also considerably increased the period between general overhauls. Other than on the Classes A3 and A4, the depot renewed components as necessary and carried out stipulated examinations at the mileages laid down.

G. Rixon

Above: The busy scene at King's Cross was recorded by the photographer on 20 June 1959 as A3 No 60067 *Ladas* is in the station loco depot a Class A1 Pacific prepares to leave with a down express. Visiting locomotives were often coaled at the station depot to save time and a visit to Top Shed. It was the practice at the station depot to ensure that the coal was of good quality and properly broken up. The passenger loco depot could be a hectic place, busier than smaller depots

about the system, although it was never classified as such. The lightweight mechanical plant was a feature for which the LNER was mainly responsible and was familiar throughout the region. The LNER, being an innovator of such ideas, installed a half ton skip hoist at the southern end of the site in about 1928, the original coaling platform being removed. The cramped nature of the site often resulted in late departures, although priority was always accorded to the main

expresses, a concept remaining from the earliest days when nothing was allowed to interfere with the running of profitable long distance trains. Today, almost everything in view except the station itself has disappeared. *T. B. Owen*

Right: Class A1 Pacific No 60123 *H. A. Ivatt* leaves King's Cross with the 3.55pm departure for Leeds on Saturday 18 August 1962. *G. Rixon*

Above: 'A4' No 60032 *Gannet* is pictured outside King's Cross (34A) MPD on 29 September 1962. Reallocated from Grantham to King's Cross on 4 June 1950, No 60032 remained at Top Shed until its closure in June 1963 when it was despatched to New England (34E) MPD from where it was quickly sent to Doncaster for a Casual Light repair. However, only three months after this visit to shops, No 60032 was withdrawn from traffic and returned to Doncaster Works for breaking. *W. Potter*

Right: Class J52 0-6-0ST No 68846, is shown outside Top Shed on 28 February 1959. Built as GNR Class J19 by Sharp Stewart & Co at Glasgow in May 1899, it was the only member of the class to carry the BR lined black livery and the only one preserved. *W. Potter*

Below: Top Shed looks somewhat empty in this 29 September 1962 view which depicts 'A4s' No 60032 *Gannet* and 60028 *Walter K.Whigham* being prepared for duty. Four years earlier in 1958, the No 1 link at King's Cross had been increased to an unprecedented total of 40 sets of men - a long way from 30 years earlier when there were only six. With such a large influx of relatively inexperienced men together with many additional long diagrams, regular manning was abandoned to the detriment of good timekeeping. However, it was to be the summer of 1961 that was recorded as being the last to see significant numbers of steam workings. Official intentions were to have Deltic power for `The Elizabethan´ non-stop run between London and Edinburgh but availability and crewing problems prevented this. Bearing in mind the run down in steam maintenance both Haymarket and King´s Cross 'A4s' put up a good showing with only one failure when No 60030 *Golden Fleece* was removed from the down train with injector trouble at Newcastle on 31 August. Of five King's Cross and three Haymarket 'A4s' used on these diagrams, pride of place must go to No 60009 *Union of South Africa,* which completed 14 consecutive return journeys between 13 August and 9 September as well as carrying the distinction of taking the last up non-stop. The last down working was hauled by No 60022 *Mallard. W. Potter*

Right: Outshopped from Doncaster Works only eight days earlier, Class A3 No 60061 *Pretty Polly* is seen back at King's Cross on 11 February 1962 after a General repair. *Hugh Ramsey*

Left: Still in immaculate condition three months after its last visit to Doncaster Works for a General Repair, King's Cross 'V2' No 60854 passes Finsbury Park signal box with an up freight in April 1962. Allocated to New England (34E) MPD when it entered traffic on 11 March 1939, No 60854 was to return to its home depot when King's Cross was losing its steam allocation in April 1963. *Geoff Rixon*

Above: Passing an impressive array of signals, Class L1 2-6-4T No 67797 works bunker-first past Hornsey signalbox with an up rake of quad-arts on 27 January 1957. The design of the quad-arts goes back before World War 1 when the GN London suburban services were operated almost entirely by rakes of antique four-wheel stock. After appointing H. N. Gresley to the position of Carriage Superintendent in 1905, it was to be 1907 before he introduced his first articulated units and it was to be a further four years before he introduced the purely suburban stock comprising eight coach trains of articulated twins. Surprisingly, after many threatened withdrawals, it was the introduction of further BR standard non-corridor stock at the end of 1965 that pre-empted the end of the quad-arts. *T. B. Owen*

Above: Many of the depot's allocation of 0-6-0 tanks appear to be 'on shed' in this view of Hornsey MPD taken on 22 September 1957. Comprising an eight road dead-end building with accommodation for approximately 40 engines and a ramped coal stage at the east side, the depot at Hornsey was opened in stages around 1899. Sited in a residential area with houses to the north, east and south, a perennial problem in steam days was that of smoke emission. After four complaints were taken out against the GNR, it was proposed either to light up the locomotives with expensive Welsh coal or defend the law suits in court. The latter course of action was taken and two cases were dismissed, but in the oth-

ers fines were imposed on the company.

Much of the traffic originating from Hornsey was in the form of goods trains which were not only run to the north of London, but also over the Thames. Much of this work was handled by the depot's 0-6-0 and 0-6-0T classes taking them to Acton, Feltham, Bricklayers Arms and Hither Green. Another of the depot's functions was to take some of the suburban load off King's Cross and by 1929 Gresley's 0-6-2T Class N2s had taken over all 10 of the shed's Metro link turns. The 'N2s' also took their turn on goods duties, particularly on trips to Mill Hill and Edgware. The end of steam traction at Hornsey was forecast in a 1957 HMSO

report, the depot closing to steam in June 1961. Diesel servicing continued at Hornsey until 1971 and in 1989 the building was still being used as a stores annexe to the new electric multiple-unit depot. *W. Potter*

Right: Also on 22 September 1957, Class J50/4 No 68990 0-6-0T is seen outside the depot. Built by the LNER in 1937, this variation of the class had a larger bunker; earlier members of the class dated back to 1913. These locomotives were extremely powerful and were designed for shunting and trip workings in the West Riding of Yorkshire where they were known as 'Ardsley' tanks. *W. Potter*

'A3' No 60103 *Flying Scotsman* heads the down 'Yorkshire Pullman' near Brookmans Park on 14 July 1959. Arguably the most famous locomotive of them all, *Flying Scotsman* completed some 2,076,000 miles in traffic and made its last run in BR revenue earning service on 14 January 1963 when it hauled the 1.15pm train from King´s Cross to Leeds. Bought from BR by Mr A. F. Pegler for £3,000, No 60103 entered Darlington Works where it was given a General repair and overhaul. Every part of the locomotive was stripped down, examined, and either renewed or replaced, its refurbished boiler coming from 'A3' No 60041 *Salmon Trout,* emerging in apple green livery as LNER No 4472. Today, after 30 years of being No 4472, it has regained its BR mantle as No 60103 and once again carries the German trough type smoke deflectors which were originally fitted in December 1961. No 60103 made its return on the Torbay Steam Railway and is currently making a tour of preserved railways in the U.K. *T. B. Owen*

Heading what could be described as a typical King's Cross suburban train, 'N2/4' No 69585 heads an up local near Brookmans Park on 28 February 1959. This variation of the 'N2' class was introduced by the LNER in 1928 and was constructed with condensing apparatus and smaller chimney for working to Moorgate, the smaller chimney being to suit the Metropolitan loading gauge. Ponderous and strangely proportioned, the 'N2s' could be identified by their outriding condenser pipes, their thudding progress through the tunnels being accentuated by their flapping filler tank lids lifting rhythmically with puffs of steam. King's Cross MPD had a large allocation of this class, all fitted with condensers which, by the operation of a flap in the blast pipe, directed exhaust steam back into the side tanks via the external pipes which are visible in this picture. The trip cock required by London Transport was situated between the first two driving wheels. Today, only one member of the class survives in its former guise as LNER No 4744 and can be seen operating on the Great Central Railway. *T. B. Owen*

Left: King's Cross 'V2' No 60862 is seen at the head of an up fitted freight near Brookmans Park on 28 February 1959. After initial allocation to Gorton when new, No 60862 spent most of her years in traffic as a King's Cross based loco and left that depot when it was preparing to close in April 1963. During a General repair at Darlington Works in September 1961 it was fitted with a Kylchap double blastpipe and chimney in addition to a Smith speedometer. *T. B. Owen*

Above: Also on 28 February 1959, '9F' 2-10-0 No 92143 is at the head of an up mineral train near Brookmans Park. The Class 9F 2-10-0s were the only really new steam locomotive concept to be introduced after Nationalisation, No 92000 being unveiled at Crewe Works in January 1954. The class was introduced to speed up unfitted block workings between New England and Ferme Park as well as similar duties on other regions. One of the 2-10-0s' most noticeable

features was the 5ft diameter driving wheels which were some 3 to 6in larger than had been normal on heavy freight engines in this country. The most powerful two-cylinder locomotive in Britain, the 2-10-0 had an axle load that was kept down to 15½ ton to give it a wide route availability. Special measures were taken to secure a particularly rigid and robust frame and to produce a thoroughly serviceable loco that was easy on maintenance. *T. B. Owen*

An extremely successful mixed traffic locomotive, Thompson's 'B1' 4-6-0 was introduced in 1942. Whilst built to a new design its construction utilised many existing components. The class eventually numbered 410, one, No 61057 being damaged beyond economic repair in March 1950. Here we see King's Cross 'B1' No 61393 hauling an up freight near Brookmans Park on 28 February 1959. A total of 59 members of the class eventually carried names, 40 of the first 41 engines being named after species of antelope. After this group of engines, other namings became somewhat haphazard and comprised mainly names of people. The last to be named, No 61379 *Mayflower*, was to celebrate the link between the towns of Boston in England and the USA. *T. B. Owen*

'A4' No 60014 *Silver Link* heads an up passenger working near Brookmans Park on 28 February 1959. Built in 1935, *Silver Link* was one of the original four 'A4s' introduced to operate the 'Silver Jubilee' express. By the early 1950s its outward appearance had changed in many respects. Its number 2509 had changed to 14 and then to 60014 and its livery had gone from grey through black, blue again, a different blue, finally being given BR lined green. All these changes were superficial, the constant feature being that at almost 25 years old, it was still working prestige trains along the East Coast main line. Visibly showing only the light exhaust of a Kylchap double chimney, No 60014 was among the first five 'A4s' to be withdrawn from traffic in December 1962. *T. B. Owen*

With the start of the 1963 summer timetable the end of steam on the GN main line was in sight as all express passenger turns were dieselised, King's Cross shed being closed after the evening of Saturday 15 June and, in theory, steam banned totally south of Hitchin and, almost so, south of Peterborough. In May 1963 'A1' Pacific No 60145 *Saint Mungo* is seen heading north through Hadley Wood with an evening train from King's Cross. During the evening of Friday 14 June no fewer than 10 out of 16 main line passenger and goods trains were steam hauled and for the last Saturday, Top Shed turned out 'A4s' Nos 60017/25 for the 9.05am to Newcastle and 9.20am 'White Rose' to Leeds, followed by 'A3s' Nos 60061/3 on the 10.10am to Leeds and 11.15am to Scarborough respectively. The final scheduled steam working to Leeds on 16 June was taken by 'A1' No 60158 of Doncaster at 10.45pm. With the closure of Top Shed its 11 'A4s' were transferred to New England (34E) MPD displacing the 'A3s' which were sent down the line to Grantham where they were joined by the surviving King's Cross 'A3s'. No 60145 with No 60124 *Kenilworth* became the last two members of the class, No 60145 taking the final working, a special from York to Newcastle on 31 December 1965. Both locomotives had survived at York where they had been kept for standby duties.

R. Hobbs

New England (34E) '9F' 2-10-0 No 92148 is passing through Hatfield station with an up freight on 20 February 1959. In its final form Hatfield station had some peculiar features: two platforms in staggered formation connected by a footbridge, providing all passenger facilities. Both had waiting rooms, the eastern one also having a small refreshment room. By 1957 the locomotive depot at Hatfield had an allocation of 24 comprising engines of Classes J52, N2 and N7. There were four 'N2' diagrams and 10 'N7' diagrams, the latter being confined to the branches, goods only to St Albans and Hertford, with mixed traffic to Luton and Dunstable. The introduction of DMUs on the King's Cross suburban lines in 1959 caused a big reduction in steam working from Hatfield shed, and diesel locomotives based at Hornsey gradually took over the remaining branch line goods turns. The depot at Hatfield closed completely on 2 January 1961. From this date forward Hatfield's role as a railway centre declined significantly following the withdrawal of all traffic from the three branches between April 1965 and January 1969 except for the working of refuse trains to Blackbridge siding which continued until 1970.
T. B. Owen

Above: Class V2 No 60871 heads an up parcels across Welwyn viaduct on 14 April 1962. When members of this class were initially fitted with BR smokebox door numberplates it became necessary to move the upper lamp iron to the top of the door. Whilst adequate for supporting a lamp it was unsuitable for carrying a headboard. It was not until 1962 that remedial measures were taken on only six members of this class to reposition the numberplate across the upper door strap and the lamp iron even lower than before. *T. B. Owen*

Right: Two weeks after receiving a General repair at Doncaster Works, Class A1 Pacific No 60139 *Sea Eagle* is seen heading a down express through Welwyn North on 14 April 1962. *T. B. Owen*

Below: Only eight days after leaving Doncaster Works following a General repair, 'A3' No 60108 *Gay Crusader* heads a down freight near Stevenage on 14 April 1962. Despite the Class A3 being some 25 to 30 years old, King's Cross shedmaster, Peter Townend, was an enthusiastic 'A3' user, and having a Doncaster upbringing, he was determined that they would not be out-shone by the new diesels that were being allocated to King's Cross in 1960. A keen locomotive engineer, he had observed steam locomotive practice whilst holidaying in West Germany and on his return gained authority for the trial fitting of trough type smoke deflectors to four members of the Class A3. The fitting of the Kylchap double chimney had given the Class A3 an extended lease of life although the problem of the softer exhaust drifting down had to be overcome by adding the trough type smoke deflectors. *T. B. Owen*

Right: On the same day, 'A4' No 60021 *Wild Swan* heads an up express also near Stevenage. By this time *Wild Swan* had undergone all modifications including the fitting of a BTH type speed indicator which it received during its final General repair in November 1961. Allocated to King's Cross in April 1950, No 60021 spent a brief spell at New England (34E) MPD before withdrawal came in October 1963. *T. B. Owen*

Above Right: 'A4' No 60007 *Sir Nigel Gresley* enters Peterborough North with the 3pm King's Cross-Newcastle express on 2 June 1962. The 100th Gresley Pacific to be constructed when completed in November 1937, No 4498 was appropriately named after its designer and painted in Garter Blue livery. No 4498 was the last of an order built with financial aid from the government which was to help reduce the number of unemployed. Today, No 4498 has been returned to its Garter Blue livery by members of the A4 Locomotive Society and one of six members of the class to be preserved, it can still be seen regularly working special trains on BR. *Peter Fitton*

Below Right: Also on 2 June 1962, 'A1' No 60156 *Great Central* enters Peterborough with the up 'Flying Scotsman'. No 60156 had taken over this train at Doncaster following the failure of a 'Deltic'. Having already made its last visit to Doncaster Works in July 1961, No 60156 had been allocated to Doncaster (36A) MPD in April 1959 and on this occasion it was acting as up side pilot when it took over the train from the failed 'Deltic'. Four members of the Class A1 were named after the constituent companies of the LNER, the nameplates being surmounted by the appropriate coat of arms. At the time of the initial naming of these locomotives in the early 1950s, the hand painting of the coat of arms was in the hands of just one man who had the skill required. The Class A1 was the final design of the LNER and built by BR after nationalisation during 1948-49. By the 1950s the weight of trains had been reduced and the emphasis was on accelerated timings. The 'A1s' carrying out these duties were operating well within their designed capacity. At a time when some of the older Pacifics were not too reliable, the Class A1 performed consistently well, running higher mileages than their predecessors and with lower maintenance costs than any other Pacifics on BR. *Peter Fitton*

Designed for high speed passenger working, the 'A4s' were equally at home in the role of high speed freight operation. Here, No 60028 *Walter K. Whigham* passes the recently constructed goods depot at Peterborough with an up fitted freight working in June 1962. Only one year earlier No 60028 was one of three 'A4s' chosen to work Royal Trains from the capital to York for the wedding of the Duke of Kent in the Minster. Whilst Nos 60003 *Andrew K. McCosh* and 60015 *Quicksilver* hauled trains carrying guests from the lower orders it was No 60028 which hauled the Queen and her personal guests. However, by December 1962 both Nos 60028 and 60003 had been withdrawn, No 60015 surviving until it too was withdrawn from King's Cross MPD in April 1963. Prior to modernisation at Peterborough there was a 20mph speed restriction through the station, all up passenger and freight trains calling at Peterborough had to be routed over one track. Also, all down freight trains calling at Peterborough had to cross the up line before they could enter New England yard and re-cross it when leaving - an intolerable inconvenience when more frequent express services were about to be introduced. *W. A. Kelsey*

Left: One of 16 Class B1 4-6-0s to enter departmental service at the end of their regular duties on BR, No 61272, bearing the inscription 'Departmental Locomotive No 25', is seen alongside the coal stage at New England MPD on 28 March 1965. After a brief spell at Top Shed at the end of 1958, No 61272 was transferred to New England MPD in April 1959, and was withdrawn two months before this picture was taken in January 1965. Following a period in store at Colwick (40E) MPD, it was despatched to Garnham, Harris & Elton at Chesterfield where it was broken up. The final closure of New England MPD came on 30 September 1968, although the diesel fuelling point remained in use until 9 March 1969 when an alternative point was opened at Spital. However, there was one occasion in 1967 when steam returned in the form of GWR 4-6-0 No 7029 *Clun Castle en route* to King's Cross to work a railtour. *W. Potter*

Below: Only weeks away from the end of its working life, a somewhat begrimed 'A3' No 60107 *Royal Lancer* heads an up Leeds express past North Tallington on 8 June 1963. Having received a Light Casual repair in January 1963, No 60107 was one of the last steam locomotives to pass through Doncaster Works, as remaining ER locomotives deemed worthy of repair were dealt with by Darlington Works. *P. Riley*

Above: Ivatt GNR designed Class C12 4-4-2T No 67357 has arrived at Essendine with the REC 'Charnwood Forester' railtour on 14 April 1957. Regular performers on the branch to Stamford, the Class C12s remained in use until they were eventually replaced by ex-GC Class N5 0-6-2Ts which dominated branch services until final closure on 15 June 1959. Today little trace remains of the GNR at Stamford although the former Midland Railway route still passes through the town. *T. B. Owen*

Right: Before receiving its Kylchap double chimney and trough type smoke deflectors, Class A3 No 60103 *Flying Scotsman* heads the down 'Norseman' up Stoke Bank near Little Bytham on 23 August 1958.

T. B. Owen

Left: Gresley 'A3' Pacific No 60107 *Royal Lancer* is approaching Stoke Tunnel with a Leeds-King's Cross express on 15 June 1963. It was a sad year for the 'A3s'. No 60107 had completed $2^1/4$ million miles in 40 years of service and was consigned to the scrap heap along with 32 classmates. *P. Riley*

Above: Class A2/3 No 60500 heads the down 'Heart of Midlothian' near Stoke Summit on 18 July 1959. The 2,000th locomotive to be constructed at Doncaster Works, it brought together Thompson's various ideas on Pacific design, and in view of his impending retirement, the LNER board allowed it to be named *Edward*

Thompson. Designated as Class A2 when completed in May 1946, it was changed to Class A2/3 by Peppercorn in April 1947. Allocated to New England (34E) MPD in June 1950, No 60500 operated from that shed for most of its working life and was withdrawn in June 1963.

T. B. Owen

Passing the marker indicating five miles from Grantham, Class A3 No 60047 *Donovan* emerges from Stoke Tunnel with the up 'Scarborough Spa Express' on 18 July 1959. Entering traffic as Class A1 No 2546 in August 1924 it was rebuilt as Class A3 in 1947, re-entering traffic in January 1948. One of the most noticeable changes when rebuilt to Class A3 was the change from right-hand to left-hand drive on those members of the class that were not already built as left-hand drive. Other differences to be noted were that engines operating over the former North British lines in Scotland were fitted with air brakes and different boiler mountings. At the time of this picture, No 60047 had not received the other major change in appearance to members of this class which was the fitting of German trough type smoke deflectors. Also clearly visible is the tender of GNR design with two coal rails all round. In July 1959, it was one of 19 of the class to be allocated to Grantham (34F) MPD, where it remained until transferred to New England (34E) MPD in August 1962. *T. B. Owen*

In this view taken at Great Ponton on 18 July 1959, Class A1 Pacific No 60128 *Bongrace* is working an up York express. The Peppercorn Class A1 Pacifics, whilst introduced by BR in 1948, were every inch 'LNER' in concept and were the mainstay of East Coast main line services in the early 1950s when the older Gresley Pacifics were having problems. Allocated to Doncaster (36A) MPD from King's Cross some three months before this picture was taken, No 60128 was to remain working from that shed until withdrawal in January 1965. Stored for two months at Doncaster, she was towed to Draper's yard in Hull where she was broken up with nine other members of the same class in April of that year. *T. B. Owen*

Above: Frodingham (36C) based Austerity 2-8-0 No 90070 heads a lengthy rake of iron ore empties, presumably bound for High Dyke, past Great Ponton on 18 July 1959. Much of the High Dyke iron ore traffic was at that time moved by Grantham's Class O2 2-8-0s which carried out their duties until that depot closed in September 1963 when the traffic was handed over to diesel traction. No 90070 was to soldier on at Frodingham until it was withdrawn in January 1965.

T. B. Owen

Right: Top Shed's spotless 'A3' No 60066 *Merry Hampton* heads an up express south of Grantham in July 1962. Clearly visible in this picture is the cab which has a prominent ventilator. This cab was fitted to 60066 in January 1948 after its own cab had been wrecked in the derailment at Goswick in October 1947. This cab started life in 1923 on Class A1 No 1481ₙ No 60066 did not have a smokebox numberplate fitted until October 1949 and by that time true *Gill Sans* sixes were in use. A wandering loco, No 60066 had been re-

allocated to King's Cross for the fifth time in November 1959 and stayed there until Top Shed closed in June 1963 when it was despatched to Grantham where it lasted for a further three months before being withdrawn from traffic. *D. Penney*

Left: An atmospheric scene at Grantham (34F) MPD in March 1959 as another of Top Shed's spotless 'A3s', No 60039 *Sandwich*, is being coaled before its next turn of duty. As with many former GNR MPDs, Grantham always suffered from restricted space. *D. Penney*

Above: Grantham's named 'B1' 4-6-0 No 61251 *Oliver Bury* stands in the platform with a down semi-fast. On 19 September 1906 Grantham was the scene of a terrible accident when at 11pm the 'Scotch Express' failed to stop and travelled through the station at 50mph.

Moments later a dreadful roar rent the Lincolnshire air as witnesses saw the terrible sight of wrecked parts of the train catching fire. Fourteen people were killed including the driver and fireman. The Railway Inspectorate was unable to find the cause. *D. Penney*

A busy scene at Grantham station in July 1960 as Heaton's Class A1 No 60132 *Marmion* departs with an up express and King's Cross 'A4' No 60008 *Dwight D. Eisenhower* waits to take over a later train. No 60008 was one of six examples of Class A4 to be preserved, being shipped to the American National Railroad Museum, Green Bay, Wisconsin, USA, in April 1964. Grantham was always used for the time-honoured practice of locomotive changing, a feature of operation which became unnecessary with the introduction of diesels. At the end of the 1963 summer timetable, the depot at Grantham closed on 9 September and it was very appropriate that two of its 'A3s' were the last locomotives to leave. No 60108 *Gay Crusader* took a down passenger working and No 60106 *Flying Fox* was despatched with a goods to Doncaster, bringing to a close 108 years of railway history. Today the southern end of the Grantham site is covered by a factory, the rest of the area being overgrown and derelict. *D. Penney*

A classic portrait of 'A3' Pacific No 60059 *Tracery* as it turns on the triangle at Grantham MPD in August 1959. In 1951 the problem of turning locomotives at Grantham was resolved at the instigation of the District Locomotive Superintendent, John Blundell. He authorised the construction of a triangle on open ground to the west of the two sheds. Even so, there was insufficient space to build a triangle 'proper', the approach tracks crossing on a scissors, an arrangement which was certainly unique in Britain. Prior to the introduction of the triangle, locomotives were turned on a 70ft turntable which in mid-1950 became inoperable owing to the collapse of the foundations under the centre pivot. After removal and refurbishment, it was eventually reinstated at Melton Constable. Whilst the turntable was out of action, locomotive turning was carried out by using the Barkston triangle, an expensive and time consuming eight-mile round trip. Built at Doncaster as a member of Class A1 in March 1925, *Tracery* was rebuilt as an 'A3' in July 1942. As visible in this picture, it was fitted with its Kylchap double chimney during a Casual Light repair at Doncaster in July 1958 and later received the German trough type smoke deflectors in September 1961. Finally withdrawn from traffic in December 1962 it had completed some 2,523,843 recorded miles. *D. Penney*

Above: Thompson Class A2/3 Pacific No 60520 *Owen Tudor* quietly leaves Grantham with a down semi-fast passenger train in April 1962.

On 7 January 1950, No 60520 headed an 11-coach express from Aberdeen near Welwyn Garden City when it was in collision with the 6.18am local passenger train from Baldock to King's Cross headed by Class L1 2-6-4T No 67741. The latter had crossed to the main line, passed the advance starter at clear and was proceeding at about 30mph when it was struck by the Aberdeen express. Although there were track magnets at distant signals between Grantham and King's Cross, No 60520 had not been fitted with the necessary cab equipment to receive the warnings. At the inquiry the driver said he had seen the outer distant at 'clear'. He had missed the outer home and did not see the inner home through the engine's steam and smoke, the locomotive ending up on its side in the ballast. *D. Penney*

Right: Class A5/1 4-6-2T No 69827 leaves Grantham yard with a lightweight goods train for the Nottingham line in April 1959. This former GCR Robinson designed class was introduced in 1911, No 69827 being one of three members of the class formerly allocated to Neasden (34E) MPD. *D. Penney*

Left: Colwick (40E) allocated Class J11 0-6-0 'Pom-Pom' No 64397 is leaving Grantham with a stopping train for Nottingham in April 1959. This former GCR Robinson designed Class 9J 0-6-0 was introduced in 1901. No 64397 was reallocated to Lincoln (40A) MPD later in 1959 and finally joined all remaining members of the class at Gorton Works where the last survivor, No 64354, arrived in October 1962. *D. Penney*

Above: Copley Hill (56C) based 'A1' Pacific No 60141

Abbotsford has just emerged from Peascliffe Tunnel with an up express in June 1961. Allocated to York when new in December 1948 and to King's Cross in October 1949, No 60141 together with Nos 60114 and 60120, all having been recently outshopped, were allocated to Copley Hill in June 1950 in exchange for their most run down 'A1s' 60128/36/44. This was to facilitate the change in Eastern Region workings which was to discontinue the changing of engines at Peterborough

and Grantham. Copley Hill then catered for seven workings to London on weekdays (more at week-ends) some of which involved overnight fitted freight trains, but apart from the up 'Yorkshire Pullman', down 'West Riding' and the up and down 'Queen of Scots', all the trains saw crew changes at Doncaster or Grantham.
D. Penney

Doncaster-based Class A1 Pacific No 60149 *Amadis* climbs the 1 in 200 of Gamston bank with an up express in June 1963. When built, all of the Class A1 Pacifics were fitted with electric lighting equipment, the Stone's turbo-generator being located inside the right-hand smoke deflector. Because of the extra maintenance involved the electric lighting was received with mixed feelings, since the oil lamps still had to be used to denote the type of train to signalmen. No 60149 was fitted with the ATC equipment in October 1949, following the resumption of testing of the Hudd type Automatic Train Control after the end of the World War 2. The large plate preventing the front coupling from swinging and causing damage to the signal receiving equipment is clearly visible below the front buffer beam. No 60149 had already received its last General repair at Doncaster Works in December 1961. Two months before this picture was taken No 60149 had made its last visit to the plant for weighing, but it was to be another year before the final call to the scrap-yard came in June 1964, *Amadis* being broken at Cox & Danks' yard at Wadsley Bridge in January 1965. *D. Penney*

BR Class J6 0-6-0 No 64174 ambles past Grove Road with a permanent way train in August 1959. Built as GNR Class J22 in 1911, the design was one of two types of superheated 0-6-0s to be introduced during Gresley's first two years as CME of the Great Northern Railway, but the class was in essence virtually an Ivatt design. Before January 1957 only two members of the 110 strong class had been withdrawn, two more following during the course of 1957 and in 1958 a further 30 were to follow. By the end of 1961 another 38 examples had gone and by 1962, their last year of service, only seven members of the class were still active, the last of these being based at Ardsley and Copley Hill MPDs.
P. J. Hughes/Colour-Rail

Left: Class V2 2-6-2 No 60852 heads south from Retford with the morning Edinburgh-King's Cross fitted freight in November 1960. Except for a three week period at Copley Hill in early 1946, No 60852 spent its entire life operating from Doncaster, from being delivered new in March 1939 until withdrawn from traffic in late September 1963. *D. Penney*

Above: During its one year allocation to King's Cross from June 1957 to September 1958, Class A1 No 60157 *Great Eastern* heads an up express out of Retford in November 1957. Five members of this class, Nos 60153-60157 were fitted with Timken roller bearings which allowed them to cover high mileages between major repairs. During its allocation to King's

Cross No 60157 was noted for rough riding at speeds over 60 mph and after examination during a non-classified repair at Doncaster Works in April 1957 it received adjustment to the weight on the bogie side control springs to rectify the problem. *D. Penney*

Below: Class A1/1 No 60113 *Great Northern* leaves Retford with an up express in October 1958. The solitary example of Class A1/1, No 60113 was officially a Thompson rebuild from the original Gresley 'A1' Pacific No 4470 of 1922, although practically nothing from the earlier locomotive was used. After its rebuilding, *Great Northern* compared well with 'A4s' in economy and performance and averaged 55,000 miles per year in traffic. When rebuilt No 4470 did not have smoke deflectors and had shallow cab sides with a straight nameplate on the smokebox. However, within three months the cab sides were altered to a more orthodox style and the nameplates were transferred to its large new smoke deflectors. *D. Penney*

Right: Whilst not strictly on a former Great Northern Railway route, Class B1 4-6-0 No 61211 departs from Retford with an all stations stopping train for Lincoln. One of five 'B1s' allocated to Retford GC (36E) MPD, No 61211 is traversing former Great Central Railway metals. *D. Penney*

Gresley Class B17/1 4-6-0 No 61647 *Helmingham Hall* stands outside Doncaster Works after receiving a General repair on 12 May 1956. At this time No 61647 retain the Lion & Wheel emblem on the tender, the new BR crest being applied to locomotives from August 1957. At first the new crest was handed (as the emblem had been) but for the lion to face to the right was unacceptable in heraldry. Alas by the time BR had decided to make amends it was too late for any of the class to be amended. The LNER Diagram Book listed the 'B17' class in six parts, No 2847 (later No 61647) being one of five engines introduced in 1935 with the GE tender and having the coupled wheel springs comprising 15 leaves, each ¹/₂in thick and 4ft long instead of 3ft 6in. The earlier locomotives built as Parts 1 & 2 were later altered to Part 3, a process completed by July 1938. When King George V died at Sandringham in January 1936, it was No 2847 that was chosen to haul the funeral train from King's Lynn to London. This was because the expected choice, No 2800 *Sandringham,* was out of action under repair at Stratford Works. *T. B. Owen*

Class K3 2-6-0 No 61906 stands outside 'The Plant' on 16 July 1961. Whilst it is seen carrying a Tyne Dock (52H) MPD shedplate, No 61906 was reallocated to Hull Dairycoates (50B) MPD later in the same month. The 'K3s' were designed by Sir Nigel Gresley, at the Doncaster Works of the Great Northern Railway, in 1920. The most prominent feature of this design was the 6ft diameter boiler, a feature not exceeded on any other locomotive in Britain. The first batch of 10 built during 1920 had the Great Northern style (almost open) cab incorporating an arched instead of a flat roof. With their Gresley-derived motion, the inside piston valves being actuated by means of a rocker arm from the outside valve spindle, the locomotives had a six-beat exhaust, typical of Gresley three-cylinder locomotives. When the GNR became part of the LNER group in 1923, it was not until 1924 that a further batch of 27 was put in hand at the Darlington Works of the former North Eastern Railway. These locomotives had the elegant NER style of double window cab, a great improvement on the GNR pattern. *T. B. Owen*

York based Thompson Pacific Class A2/2 No 60501 *Cock o' the North* stands next to the coaling plant at Doncaster (36A) MPD on 20 April 1958. One of six locomotives rebuilt from Class P2 2-8-2s, No 60501 was the last to receive LNER green livery in March 1948, though with BRITISH RAILWAYS on its tender. Whilst the original 2-8-2s were believed to suffer from many defects, Thompson's Pacific version turned out to have just as many drawbacks. Not only did the Pacifics look wrong, the front end arrangement required additional maintenance which resulted in further strengthening of the frames between the inside and outside cylinders. No 60501 was to remain allocated to York MPD until withdrawn in February 1960.
W. Potter

Former GNR designed locomotives feature strongly in this general view of Doncaster (36A) MPD also taken on 20 April 1958. At the heart of the GNR empire, and later the LNER, Doncaster Carr MPD is situated on the east side of the line, south of the station. First records indicate that the first building was erected by September 1849 and consisted of a single-road wooden structure. This early temporary building was quickly replaced with a much larger construction with four hipped roofs covering three roads. By the 1880s the GNR concentrated on building sheds with roofs of the 'Northlight' pattern which had become commonplace on many other railways. The provision of mechanical coalers was not introduced by the Great Northern, but by the LNER. The massive 500 ton capacity coal hopper at Doncaster was soon christened 'The Cenotaph'. This coaling stage, erected in the 1920s, was powered by electricity and operated by lifting a full wagon of coal to the top of the tower, tipping the contents into a bunker, enabling up to four engines to be coaled simultaneously. To keep down dust, automatic slakers were positioned at strategic points, a particularly useful feature for occupants of neighbouring dwellings. *W. Potter*

Above: Ex-works '9F' 2-10-0 No 92177 stands outside Doncaster MPD on 20 April 1958. Allocated when new to New England (34E) MPD, it spent all of its working life at that depot, excepting for a few months in store at Langwith Junction (41J) MPD in 1965. *W. Potter*

Right: Also ex-works at Doncaster on that day was named Class B1 4-6-0 No 61036 *Ralph Assheton*. Introduced by Thompson in 1942, the 'B1' class formed the highest number of 4-6-0s on the LNER. Popular and versatile locos, they could be seen at the head of all but the fastest expresses. The first to be withdrawn was No 61085 from Leicester (GC) MPD in December 1961. No 61036 staying allocated to Doncaster until withdrawn in September 1962. *W. Potter*

Class A3 No 60082 *Neil Gow* is outside Doncaster MPD on 31 August 1961, one week after leaving 'The Plant' where it had received a General repair. During this visit to works No 60082 had received the boiler previously carried by 'A4' No 60022 *Mallard*. Although still carrying the shedplate from its former depot at Leeds Holbeck (55A), it had been officially allocated to Heaton (52B) MPD on 16 July 1961. From the latter date until withdrawal in September 1963, No 60082 shuttled between Gateshead (52A) and Heaton (52B) MPDs, seeing very little use since its major overhaul. *G. W. Morrison*

Immortal star of the film the 'Elizabethan', 'A4' Pacific No 60017 *Silver Fox* leaves Doncaster with an express passenger for King's Cross on Sunday 29 April 1962. A regular performer on the non-stop London-Edinburgh workings which re-commenced in the form of the 'Elizabethan' in June 1953, the locomotives working the 392 miles in six and a half hours. When No 60017 received the BR green livery, the stainless steel boiler straps and cab window frames were painted over, only the two foxes remaining uncovered. On another visit to works in May 1957, No 60017 got the benefit of a Kylchap double blastpipe and chimney and was also one of the first 'A4s' to change from the BR emblem to the crest. Apart from a short spell at New England (34E) after King's Cross MPD had closed, *Silver Fox* was always allocated to 'Top Shed'. *G. W. Morrison*

Members of the 289-strong Class J39 0-6-0, introduced by Gresley in 1926, were allocated throughout the Eastern, North Eastern and Scottish Regions of BR. Found operating on both freight and passenger trains, the class remained intact until May 1959. Here, No 64796, allocated to Ardsley (56B) MPD, passes through Wakefield Westgate with a down mineral train on 24 August 1961. No 64796 became one of the last members of the class in operation, being withdrawn in December 1962. *G. W. Morrison*

Shortly after leaving Doncaster Works where it had received its last General repair, Peppercorn Class A1 Pacific No 60146 *Peregrine* is passing Beeston Junction, Leeds, with a running-in turn from Leeds Central to Doncaster on 5 June 1962. Throughout the 1950s accident inspectors had often concluded that drivers misjudged the speed of their locomotive. It seemed necessary to ascertain the accurate speed of a train and during the 1950s all 49 'A1' Pacifics were fitted with a Smith-Stone speed indicator. This was driven off the left-hand rear coupling pin, where no additional support bracket was required. Whilst all Class A1 locomotives were originally fitted with electric lighting equipment, it can be noted that No 60146 is one of those members of the class from which it was removed. Entering traffic in April 1949, *Peregrine* was initially allocated to Doncaster (36A) MPD and was transferred to Copley Hill (37B) MPD for only two months commencing 30 April 1950 before being transferred to York. Except for a three month period in 1963, No 60146 remained allocated to York until it was withdrawn from traffic in October 1965 and was sold for scrap to T. W. Ward at Killamarsh. *G. W. Morrison*

'A4' No 60017 *Silver Fox* heads the up 'White Rose' past Wortley South Junction on 5 April 1962. At this point the train is crossing over the former LNWR line from Leeds to Huddersfield and Manchester. By July 1962 timetables for the Great Northern line of the Eastern Region were being compiled, not by an army of timetable clerks, but by a single electronic computer installed in Great Northern House. Previously, the task of compiling the GN main line timetable, from Broad Street, Moorgate and King's Cross as far as Shaftholme Junction, took some 2,000 man hours. The new computer meant that the job could be done by two girls feeding in information for a week, followed by 30 hours of computer time. It was estimated that it would take a similar time to produce timetables for the Sheffield and Lincolnshire districts. The Pegasus computer required to carry out these functions was supplied by Ferranti, the project being initiated as early as August 1957 and was encouraged at first by Mr G. F. Fiennes and later Mr J. Bonham-Carter, successive Line Traffic Managers of the GN line. At the time of its introduction, the Pegasus computer produced what was the world's first co-ordinated timetable for an area of railway. *G. W. Morrison*

Class A1 Pacific No 60118 *Archibald Sturrock* passes its home depot at Copley Hill (56C) with the up 'Yorkshire Pullman' on 11 May 1961. No 60118 was one of three Class A1 locomotives delivered brand-new to Copley Hill in November 1948, the others being No 60119 *Patrick Stirling* and 60134 *Foxhunter*. The new style Pullman cars, of which four examples can be seen behind the loco, were introduced in September 1960 and were constructed by the Metropolitan-Cammell Co of Saltley, Birmingham, and cost approximately £17,000 each. The 44 new Pullmans for the East Coast route were designed by the Pullman Car Co, the first four vehicles being placed in the King's Cross-Sheffield Pullman on 28 September 1960. Once introduced, some of the existing prewar Pullmans were transferred to the Southern Region and were refurbished at Preston Park works before they replaced the 52 wooden-bodied cars still working south of the Thames. The first of the Southern Region trains to be re-equipped by the deported East Coast cars was the 'Bournemouth Belle' being closely followed by the Ocean Liner boat trains.

G. W. Morrison

Immaculate King's Cross 'A4' No 60025 *Falcon* departs from Leeds Central with the 12.30pm to King's Cross on 24 April 1961. No 60025 spent 22 of its 26 years' life allocated to King's Cross and was one of the favourites for hauling the most important named trains. The cleanliness of *Falcon* is a tribute to the enthusiasm of King's Cross shedmaster, Peter Townend, and of Dick Ball, his chargeman cleaner. Curiously on this day No 60025 is not carrying its 34A shedplate.

On 17 May 1967 the remodelled station at Leeds City was opened when a commemorative plaque was unveiled by the Lord Mayor. Three new connections enabled all passenger traffic to be diverted into City, and Central station was closed. A century earlier Leeds was served by six railway companies working into five main stations. Services from Bradford Exchange and King's Cross were diverted from Holbeck Junction near the old Holbeck High Level Station by a curve on a new alignment down to Whitehall Junction, joining the Skipton line into City Station. *G. W. Morrison*

Class A3 No 60108 *Gay Crusader* awaits departure from Leeds Central with the 12.30pm departure to King's Cross on 16 May 1961. Only three weeks earlier No 60108 had visited 'The Plant' for a Casual Light repair having received its double chimney during a General repair in May 1959. It was not until November 1961 that the German type smoke deflectors were fitted to *Gay Crusader*. Re-allocated to King's Cross in November 1958, No 60108 was allocated to New England (34E), Grantham (34F) and Doncaster (36A)

MPDs before final withdrawal came in October 1963.

Prior to July 1930 Pacifics were not allowed to work between Doncaster and Leeds (Central) and it was a further six years before their appearance on this line became regular. At that time Doncaster shed sent Class A1s Nos 2553 *Prince of Wales* and 2555 *Centenary* to Copley Hill MPD, mainly to work the 'Queen of Scots' Pullman trains to and from the capital. *G. W. Morrison*

Below: Stanier Class 5 No 44942 passes Laisterdyke with the Bradford portion of the 'Yorkshire Pullman', 9.55am from Bradford to Leeds City, on 13 June 1967. With the closure of Leeds Central station on 30 April 1967 Bradford portions of trains from King's Cross were no longer detached at Wakefield, when they had been worked directly to Bradford. *Peter Fitton*

Right: Low Moor's Stanier 2-6-4T No 42616 passes Laisterdyke with the 11.00am Bradford Exchange-King's Cross on 29 May 1967. No 42616 had only recently been reallocated from Birkenhead (8H) MPD where it had seen use on Birkenhead-Chester services. A former Great Northern Railway water column can be seen on the end of the platform. The swan-neck enabled

locomotives with high-sided tenders to fill up. For several years prior to the end of steam traction, London Midland 2-6-4Ts of both Fairburn and Stanier patterns were employed on the former GN route between Leeds and Bradford. *Peter Fitton*

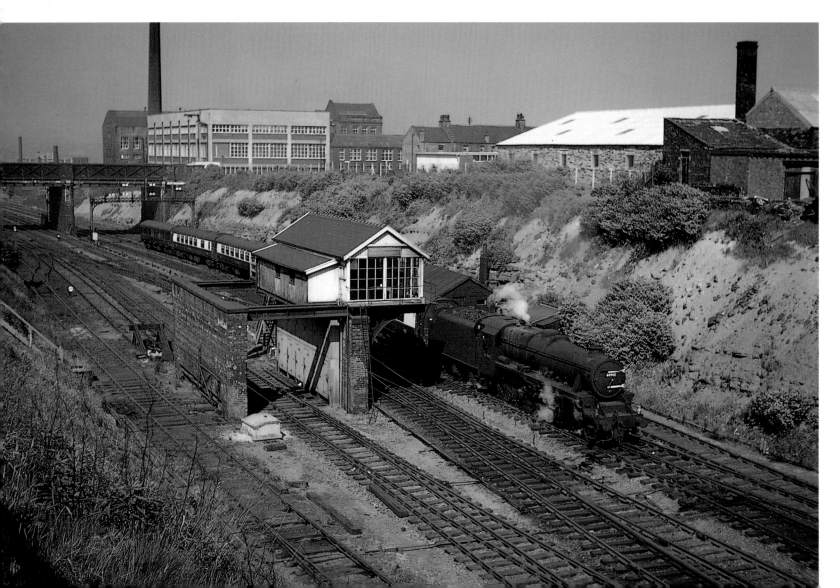

Left: Fairburn 2-6-4T No 42196 rounds the curve at St Dunstan's Junction with the 9am Bradford Exchange-King's Cross service on 16 September 1966. This train was being worked directly to Wakefield Westgate where it would be coupled to the portion from Leeds. Having spent much of its working life in Scotland, No 42196 was re-allocated from Dumfries (67E) to Leeds Neville Hill in October 1963 and was later sent to Low Moor (56F) in June 1966 from where it operated until withdrawn in May 1967. In the early 1950s many of the Bradford portions of King's Cross trains had been in the hands of former GNR Class N1 0-6-2Ts. *Peter Fitton*

Right: Recently re-allocated from Leeds Holbeck (55A) MPD, where it had spent much of its working life, to Low Moor (56F) MPD Stanier Class 5 No 44662 works past St Dunstan's Junction with the 9.55am 'Yorkshire Pullman' from Bradford Exchange to King's Cross on 25 July 1967. This was to be the last summer of steam operation on this service, the final working being on 30 September. *Peter Fitton*

Left: Fairburn 2-6-4Ts Nos 42066 and 42073 blast up the 1 in 50 out of Bradford Exchange with an 9.40am excursion to Bridlington on Whit Monday, 25 May 1967. The 2-6-4Ts would have worked the train as far as Leeds City. No 42066 was to survive for a further four months at Low Moor (56F) MPD, No 42073 being transferred from Low Moor to Normanton (55E) MPD in June 1967 where it was withdrawn from traffic. Periods in store at Mirfield and Carnforth followed before it was reprieved and is now one of two members of the class preserved on the Lakeside & Haverthwaite Railway. *Peter Fitton*

Right: Class B1 No 61030 leaves Bradford Exchange with the 3.5pm service to King's Cross on 10 September 1966. Together with Nos 61306 and 61337, No 61030 was one of the last three members of the class to survive, all being allocated to Low Moor (56F) MPD. It was to be sister locomotive No 61306 which had the honour of hauling the last steam-hauled 'Yorkshire Pullman' on 30 September 1967, all three locomotives being withdrawn from traffic from that date. Happily No 61306 was preserved and now operates with the name *Mayflower. Peter Fitton*

Ex-WD 2-8-0 No 90437 is at the head of a westbound freight through the ex-GNR station at Bottesford, between Nottingham and Grantham, on 22 December 1962. In the background behind the train is a former GNR somersault signal. Unlike conventional semaphores, where the spectacle plate is integral with the arm, the arm on the GNR somersault was balanced on a bracket jutting outwards from the signal post and was connected through a linkage to the spectacle plate, the plate itself being pivoted on the outside of the post. Whilst the signal resembled a conventional one in the on position, the arm, when in the off position, pointed almost straight down. This style of signal was introduced following an accident at Abbots Ripton in 1876 when 13 passengers were killed and 53 were injured, the accident being attributed to the fact that a slotted signal had been clogged by snow. Thus prompting the design of a better form of instrument where the semaphore arm operated well clear of the post. Whilst the year 1968 saw the demise of steam operation on British Rail, many other artefacts of the 'traditional' railway have survived much longer and up until the 1980s, old and new could be seen side by side. *Paul Riley*

One of Colwick (40E) MPD's somewhat unkempt Class O1 2-8-0s, No 63663 makes an impressive sight as it powers a freight train past the former GNR signalbox at Elton & Orston between Grantham and Nottingham on 22 December 1962. Originally built by Kitson in 1918 as ROD No 1625, this locomotive saw use on the Great Western Railway when it carried the temporary number 3074. No 1625 was one of many such engines on temporary loan to the GWR for approximately two years and when returned they were collected in large dumps at Tattenham Corner, Birkenhead and Gretna, in addition to various locations in North Wales. When first taken into LNER stock the locomotive carried the number 6359. Eventually rebuilt as part of a programme that ran between 1944 and 1952 when it was fitted with a type 100A1 boiler and was designated Class O1. As BR No 63663, it spent less than a year allocated to Colwick MPD before it was returned to Staveley GC (41H) MPD in June 1963. It was to see more than a year in traffic at the latter depot before it was withdrawn in November 1964. *Paul Riley*

Below: Gresley 'K3' 2-6-0 No 61807 heads a Sheffield-Skegness train over the Durham Ox level crossing at Lincoln in 1956. Until 1946 the Class K3 bore various numbers, depending on which were vacant at the time of construction. In that year a complete scheme of renumbering of all LNER engines was put in hand and under this scheme the 'K3s' became Nos 1800-1992 and, later, BR Nos 61800-61992. *J. F. Henton/Colour-Rail*

Right: BR Standard Britannia Pacific No 70008 *Black Prince* awaits departure from Spalding with a Grimsby-King's Cross express on Saturday 28 May 1961. Delivered to the Great Eastern section when new No 70008 was allocated to Norwich (32A) MPD and spent two years allocated to March (31B) before leaving the Eastern Region for good when it was sent to Carlisle Kingmoor (12A) MPD in December 1963. Whilst the locomotive is none too clean, the first coach is an excellent example of a BR Mk 1 carriage in the attractive plum and spilt milk livery. Today it is pleasing to note that the original station dating back to 1848 has escaped the hands of the developers and possesses a clear public address system delivered in a rich Lincolnshire accent.

Hugh Ramsey

-Left: Removed from exhibition at the National Railway Museum to the Museum annex in April 1977, Great Northern Railway 4-4-2 No 990 *Henry Oakley* was later hauled to the Keighley & Worth Valley Railway by BR Class 9F 2-10-0 No 92220 *Evening Star.* No 92220 subsequently returned to York with ex-LMS 'Crab' 2-6-0 No 42700 from the KWVR. *Henry Oakley* made its first revenue earning trip on 1 June 1977 when it piloted LMS Class 5 4-6-0 No 45212. Later that month No 990 is seen with a regular service train between Keighley and Ingrow.

Derek Huntriss

Right: BR Class J52 No 68846 was one of the first privately purchased ex-BR locomotives to be preserved in the UK. After restoration to its former identity as GNR Class J13 No 1247 it hauled an early railtour from London Bridge to Sheffield Park on 1 April 1962 when the train was joined at Horsted Keynes by none other than the late Dr Beeching who had been invited to open a new halt on the recently reopened Bluebell Railway. Here Captain Smith's GNR saddle tank is depicted at work on the North Yorkshire Moors Railway in August 1976 on the climb from Grosmont to Goathland.

Derek Huntriss

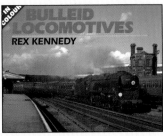

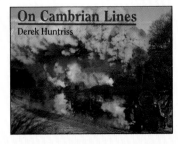